sWeet sWeat
& other poems

HYSTERICAL BOOKS

& other poems

Shane Allison

HYSTERICAL BOOKS
TALLAHASSEE, FL 2019

Copyright © Shane Allison 2019
All rights reserved under
International and Pan-American Copyright Conventions.

No portion of this book may be reproduced in any form without the written permission of the publisher, except by a reviewer, who may quote brief passages in connection with a review for a magazine or newspaper.

Sweet Sweat by Shane Allison — First Edition

Cover Image: Shane Allison
Design, production: Jay Snodgrass

ISBN — 978-0-940821-12-5
Library of Congress Cataloging Card Number —2019943621

Hysterical Books is dedicated wholly to the publication and appreciation of fine poetry and other literary genres.

HYSTERICAL BOOKS
1506 Wekewa Nene
Tallahassee Florida

Published in the United States by Hysterical Books
Tallahassee, Florida • First Edition, 2019
hystericalbooks.com
hystericalbooks@gmail.com

For Vytautas Pliura
I love and miss you.

Contents

3	BUSCH GARDENS PHOTO
4	WHEN IT COMES TO MY PARENTS, I'M A SECRET AGENT
5	A DREAM
6	THINK YOU SHOULD KNOW
8	SWEET SWEAT
9	BLACK JANITOR
11	PAUL
12	KISS ME, JOHN BEFORE YOUR WIFE COMES HOME
14	HE ATE MY SWEATY ASS
15	A MARRIED MAN
16	THEY KNOW
17	WHITE BOY
18	BASTARD
21	ASSHOLE
22	CUTE
23	JESUS GAVE ME A BLOW JOB
26	PISSING
27	I
31	SOMETHING DIRTY FOR OMAR
32	YOU ARE NOTHING TO ME
33	KICKING AND SCREAMING
35	ARMED AND DANGEROUS
37	BLACK AND GAY
38	LOST LAKE
39	TONIGHT I'M ERIK ESTRADA

42	ANGRY SESTINA TO CHRIS
44	HE SAID HE WANTED TO GET NAKED WITH ME
45	INVISIBLE
46	SUCK MY DICK
48	FLESH
49	JAIME
50	ANDY
52	PACHINKO POEM
54	DOUG
55	LATE LAST NIGHT
56	CUTE MIDDLE EASTERN BOY
61	POEM FOR CRAIG KILBORN
62	BLACK PORNO POEM
66	WHAT I REMEMBER ABOUT JARRET
68	I WANT TO BE REINCARNATED AS YOUR JEANS
69	THOSE WERE THE DAYS
70	PUNK ASS
72	ALAN
73	HIGH SCHOOL EPITHALAMION
76	TODD'S WIFE, KERRY
78	RECIPROCATE
81	WHAT I REMEMBER ABOUT CHRIS
85	NEW YORK KICKED MY ASS
87	I DREAMT
95	ON DREAMING OF KYLE SECOR NAKED WHEN TERRORISTS FLEW A PLANE INTO THE WORLD TRADE CENTER

sWeet sWeat

BUSCH GARDENS PHOTO

I was so fat in this picture.
The flip-flops hurt between my toes.
I hated that yellow shirt, but loved those shorts.
Now I hate those shorts.
I've put on more weight since then.
Couldn't have been any more than fifteen in this picture.
It was so hot that day.
I don't know what kinds of flowers those were.
My thighs are huge.
I have flat feet.
Today, I would never wear open toe sandals.
My sister was so young then.
We used to be so close.
I was very protective of her.
That's a box of camera film in my hand.
There weren't any pockets on those shorts.
The buttons on that shirt were rubber.
My hair grew back.
I can't believe how fat I was even then.
I couldn't' wear cool clothes like other teenagers.
I would have done anything for a pair of penny loafers.
I had fat arms. I hate my arms.
It was the early nineties.
This was before a bad perm took my sister's hair out.
It was before the summer vacations ended
And all the trouble began.

WHEN IT COMES TO MY PARENTS, I'M A SECRET AGENT

Shoving gay porn magazines underneath a sunken mattress.
Poems like this are written and read behind closed doors,
Locked in night stands made of real oak.
Men moaning in gay porn videos
Are turned down to a whisper in case Mama walks by.
When I was fourteen, I almost got caught by my sister jacking off.
I have learned to lock doors since then.
If I feel someone walking throughout the house
In the middle of the night, the Play Boy channel becomes the Food Network.
My phone conversations are bugged, there are hidden cameras
Throughout, in every corner, behind every mirror and figurine.
Mama waits up for me at three in the morning
 In a built in porch, sitting in her rocking chair.
"Boy, where have you been?"
There's no sneaking in this house.
I can't get away with a damn thing.
When it comes to my parents, I'm under full investigation.

A DREAM

Use to wonder late at night

Boxers or briefs

Or just your naked

Chocolate ass

Under JC Penney Sheets.

THINK YOU SHOULD KNOW

Think you should know that it's 3 a.m. and I haven't jacked off all day.
Think you should know that I occupy a double room on 84 William St.
All to myself.
Think you should know that when my Korean roommates
Are next door in the double loft area sound asleep,
I like to dance naked to George Michael songs.
Think you should know that right now, right this minute,
I'm lying in a lower bunk with my Fruit of the Looms
Up around my ankles. I think it's important to let you know
My legs are spread apart like knitting needles hiked above me.
Think you should know that I'm caressing my balls.
I'm not sure, but I think cum is swirling around in my ball sac.
Think you need to know that as I lie here exploring myself with fingers,
I can feel tiny hairs in the dark honey comb of my butt.
Think you should know that my dick is beating against my belly.
Think you should be aware that my feet are touching the railings
At the bottom of my top bunk.
Think you should know that my butthole has grown wet
Thinking about your dick at my asshole.
Just think you should know that I'm tight down there.
Think you should know that I'm playing with myself
On these navy-blue bed sheets.
Just want you to know that I'm thinking of you standing
Naked at my face.
Think you should know that there's nothing I find cuter
Than a dick with foreskin, baby.
Central air-conditioning blows up my ass.
I just want you to know that I've been thinking lately,
About your Carolina dick.

Think you should know that I worship dicks with dick cheese.
Did you know that I have yet to discover any Big Apple dick?
I think you need to know that if I don't get some dick pretty soon,
I'm going to be one more pissed off fag.
Just want you to know that if I don't get laid before I die,
I'm going to be a pissed off queer angel. A dick ring for a halo.
Think you should be aware that the naked photos are in the mail.
Think you should know that I wait for yours just the same.
Think you should know that I stuck my finger up my butt
And took a whiff of the inner me.
I think you should know that men hold hands in New York.
I think you should know that a Latino man got beat in the head
For being a queen in Queens.
I think you should know I saw a bald guy with a high-tight ass
Walking down 13th Street
Think you should know that jacking off
Only goes so far with me before I start grabbing the random asses
Of men, randomly.
Think you should know that the glory holes here are as big as watermelons.
I think you should know that I wish you were here.
I think you should know I'm holding a special place
For you in my tawdry ass, so when you come, I'll be naked and waiting.
Think you should know that I'm a virgin.

SWEET SWEAT

Do you love how a man's underwear smells after a long day
Or after a sweaty workout at the gym?
Would you like to get a package in the mail
With a pair of mine to sniff while you beat off

After a sweaty workout at the gym?
I'm very handsome with blue eyes and brown hair
With a nasty pair of underwear for you to sniff while you jack off.
I've got a 7-inch dick with a pair of hefty nuts.

Men can't resist my blue eyes and brown hair
Or my stained underwear
That houses my dick and big balls.
I take a sandwich bag with me to the gym,

And after a workout, deposit my stinkin' briefs into it.
I send them off for you to wear, wipe up your jizz with.
An airtight sandwich bag to keep in the freshness of my rank nuts.
Sound hot? Drop me a line, this offer won't last, they're going fast.

You can wear them, wipe up your cum, whatever you like
But I gotta let you know that it's gonna cost you.
Trust me, it's a good deal, my underwear is selling fast, so don't delay.
You are going to love how my balls smell.

BLACK JANITOR

Come here in your navy sweat shirt,
Green pants around your pitch-black ankles.
Forget about the wife and kids and come to me.

Haven't we met?
Haven't I seen you here before?
You're the cute black janitor

All the gay boys talk about.
Messages about you are sketched in green
And yellow paint on the walls of stalls.

Where is that black dude with the uncut cock?
Gay Janitor gives the best head.
Oh yeah, he's good.

Look at me when I'm talking to you.
I want to blow you in the front seat
Of your lime-green Cadillac.

Bend over.
I want to stuff your chocolate ass
Like a Thanksgiving turkey.

Meet me on the first floor.
There's a hole more glorious
Than drag queens to stuff your dick through.

You can wipe your cum on the sleeve
Of my corduroy coat.
I write my phone number on two-ply tissue paper.

I stick it in his back pocket.
"Here's my number, call me if you want to hang out,
Drink a few beers and have your dick sucked."

Four-eyed fat boy wants to rim the remnants
Of a bubble butt
Of a cute black janitor.

PAUL

I think about the night I fingered your butt
What you said before my tongue became my finger up your butt.
You said before I shoved my finger up your butt,
"Can I go to the bathroom before you do that?"

KISS ME, JOHN BEFORE YOUR WIFE COMES HOME

Kiss me, John before your wife comes home.
Let's make love on a floor of pizza boxes,
Hands beneath your red Polo shirt.
Come on, baby, give me something to remember you by.

Let's make love on a floor of empty pizza boxes,
Drink cream soda out of champagne glasses.
Come on, baby, give me something to remember you by
Before your wife gets home.

Drink cream soda out of champagne glasses
As we sit eating Hungry Howie's pizza on your flower-printed sofa.
Before your wife gets home,
I want to feel your beard against my face

As we sit eating Hungry Howies pizza on your flower-printed sofa,
Fingers traipsing through your jungle of brunet chest hair,
Your sand paper beard against my face.
I want your pubes to tickle my nose

As fingers play in your jungle of brunet chest hair.
I've waited to place myself between your ivory thighs,
Shorts pushed to pink ankles,
Black pubes tickle my nose.

Sink my teeth in your ass cheeks, John,
Give you a blow job during the director's cut of Star Wars,
Taste your cream soda,
Sink my teeth in your ass cheeks
Before your wife comes home.

HE ATE MY SWEATY ASS

He was eating my sweaty ass
As he was eating my sweaty ass
He said it was too sweaty
He said it was too sweaty, my sweaty ass he ate
My ass he was eating, he said it was too sweaty
My ass that he ate and licked, he said it was too sweaty
My sweaty ass he licked, he said was too sweaty
He sucked my dick before he ate and licked my ass
He sucked my dick perpendicular to my sweaty ass he licked and ate
He sucked my dick, called me daddy and said my ass was too sweaty
The same guy who sucked my dick, who ate my ass that was too sweaty,
Called me daddy
He sucked my dick, ate my ass, which he said was too sweaty
And had the balls to call me daddy
His dick sucks sucked
He sucked at dick sucking but not at ass-eating
His dick sucking sucked but he didn't suck at eating my ass
That he said was too sweaty
He ate my sweaty ass that he said was too sweaty
He sucked and licked my dick and ass that he said was too sweaty
My ass being too sweaty not my dick that he licked and sucked
While he called me daddy and ate my sweaty ass

A MARRIED MAN

He might be married, but he gives the best blow jobs.
He's had me three times:
Once on a root beer-colored picnic bench
In Tom Brown Park

The bathroom of Bellamy Hall
In a patch of blackberries off
Sam Allen Road after he made two other guys
Cum.

When he was done with me, when I
Exploded in the dirt, he said I was nice.
He must have meant the meat between my legs.
I stared at his wedding ring while I fucked his mouth

And thought of how in the dark his wife must be.
How she must worry and wonder where he goes on those
Sunday afternoons.
Instead of sucking tits, he's sucking dick.

Loves to slob on some guy's knob.

Instead of eating southern pussy,
He's biting into some dude's ass like it was a biscuit.
He might be married, but he loves the sensation of another
Man's cock in his mouth.

I have dry saliva on my dick to prove it.

THEY KNOW

Samantha knows.
I think Desirae knows but I'm not sure.
I'm sure Stephen knows.
Dave knows.
Alexis, she knows.
With the way I've been acting, I'm sure Ben knows.
Lindsey only suspects and Judy doesn't have a clue.
Cole and I have a past so of course he knows.
Both Shanna and Danielle know.
I wonder if Amanda knows.
Alex has always known.
Jeremy was the first I told while Kristi was the first to figure it out.
I wonder if O'Carl knows. He probably does, which would explain why he never talks to me.
I'm sure Cayla knows.
Wait a minute, does Nat know? And if he knows, who told him?
Maybe he figured it out. Maybe there's just something about me.
Does that new girl, Allie know?
Mike knows, but does anyone know about Mike and me?
Darryl doesn't know. No one talks to Darryl.
If Alan knows then Rachel knows.
I see the way Darrius looks at me. Someone must have told him, but who?
If John knows then Sara knows and if Sara knows then Joey knows and if Joey knows then Chris knows
And now I ain't safe no place.

WHITE BOY

Sit in the park in your snow-white Saab
Dick slumped out of the copper zipper of your khaki shorts
Shirt unbuttoned
Strawberry-red chest hair
A black boy's lips thrown around a well-to-do dick
Fingers slum your privileged ass
Your hand pushing, pressing
"You like that, nigger?"
Hot white seed down my gullet
You use fast food napkins to wipe away your shame
You thank me for getting you off
I step out of your cum-white Saab
With the aftertaste of your superiority on my tongue

BASTARD

I gave you the best moments of my life in apartment 311.
And to think I bothered writing down your number

on that torn slip of yellow legal paper
Copied from the toilet of Robert Strozier Library.

Shove it into the pocket of my jeans like loose change.
To think I almost pulled a muscle for the emotions I invested in you.

You don't want me. I'm not your ideal guy.
I'm no Prince Charming.

I'm nothing but a hard, black dick
Going in and out of your sand-toned ass.

I thought I was the queer boy that struck that nerve,
The nigger you were looking for on gay hook up apps.

You answered the door in a tee shirt that was long enough
To hang over your dick softer than cotton candy.

Walked into that living-room, ironing board sitting in the kitchen,
An unmade bed past the hallway.

I could see the gas station where you work
From the window of your place.

Gas pumps and streetlights looked like miniature toys.
"Make yourself comfortable," you said.

Took off my corduroy coat, the one I wore for slumming.
Could feel my cock swelling like a microwaved sausage

In my jeans. "Want something to drink?" you asked.
"No, I'm cool." You took your rightful place next to me, stark naked.

I unbuttoned my plaid shirt, giving chest hairs some air,
Peeled off the Levis from my legs like dead skin.

My thighs were French doors opening to your mouth.
Commercials from your television danced in my eyes

As you went in searching for oyster pearls of semen.
I rubbed your head like a crystal ball.

Then there was your butt: domed and pimpled.
Reached around, could feel a tinge of lubricated

Jelly between those ivory cheeks.
You sat upon me, roosted on my dick like a pigeon.

"Give me that black dick," you said.
"Gonna ride this big black cock."

Spewed a milk truck of spunk in your rump.
You rolled up off me like the rubber I was too lazy to grab for.

Walked naked, red and sweating to that cardboard box of a kitchen.
"I'll get you a rag for the mess," you said.

Sat exhausted at the foot of your sofa. Dick smudged
With shit. The rag was wet with water from your kitchen sink.

You had the decency to use a little soap.
A week later I dropped by that gas mart.

"Five dollars at pump 3," I said. You took my money
With a nonchalant look on your face like you had never

Seen me before, like you never gave me head that Saturday.
I feel like a notch on your bedpost.

Tried calling you, but all I got was your answering machine.
Went by, knocked on the door of apartment 311, but no luck.

I knew you were home. Could see *Sixteen Candles*
From the vertical blinds playing on your TV.

I wanted to blow your house in.
Torch the fucker; throw a brick through the window.

Take spray paint to that door you hid so cowardly behind
Writing BASTARD in big, hot pink letters.

I wanted to tell you to your face that you were an asshole,
But I just went home, grabbed a permanent marker and permanently

Wiped you out of my
Winnie the Pooh address book.

ASSHOLE

When he said to me, "My ass itches,"
Do you know what I said to him when he said, "My ass itches?"
I said to him when he said, "My ass itches,"
I said, "That's because you have a dirty ass, asshole."

CUTE

You in pitch black Chuck Taylor's,
Khaki's cuffed at your ankles.
I see you gazing at girls.
Stare at your lips smeared with Chap Stick.
I see myself in your autumn eyes.
I want to be your cold-blooded boyfriend
Beneath electric blankets
Who leaves you naked in a doublewide bed at Motel 6.

JESUS GAVE ME A BLOW JOB

In the front seat of my Toyota Celica.
It was a miracle.
He was beautiful.
I ejaculated in his almighty beard.
Slipped my phone number
In his crown of thorns.
His head fit like latex gloves
Between my legs.
"I'll call you later," he said.
I can tell he's not the type to forget faces.
He called the next morning.
"Last night was great.
I want to see you again."
He asked how my day was
And if I got the green boots I wanted.
"If you need anything at all don't hesitate to call," he said.
This was very generous of Jesus.
He asked if my mother
Was still being a pain in the ass and
If my father knows I'm happy,
Healthy and making money.
He said, "I like men who love to take it up the ass."
I found out he's been married for twenty years.
A son in the army.
A daughter with a degree in Advertising,
Children of her own.
Calling him would be impossible.
So I settled for head in the front seat
Of a black Celica in the parking lot

Of a shopping mall after closing.
The windows up,
The radio turned down like the Levis
Around my ankles.
His tongue is a roller coaster
Down the track
Of my throat in a seedy hotel with HBO
And the Playboy channel.
Come on baby,
Give me some quarters
For the vibrating bed
That sits on olive green shag
Carpet that smells like stale piss
Owned by a fat, over weight Mexican
Whose English is jagged,
Whose hands are tinged with
Kerosene from the heater in his
Bedroom around the corner
From the lobby decorated
With a black and white 50 inch TV,
Orange sofas and wallpaper coming
Undone when the glue cracks & bulks
Falling to the floor.
Where the cock roaches are bigger
Than my thumb, and rats live on lobster,
Sleeping in queen sized beds.
He plans to leave his wife.
He wants to spend the rest of his life

Feeding me grapes in bed
While we watch *Game of Thrones*.
Let's run away together in your 64 Thunderbird to Las Vegas
For a quick wedding where the justice of the peace
Is an Elvis impersonator.
Bible in one hand, fried peanut butter and banana sandwich in the other.
Jesus said, "I can't leave my children.
My wife wants things like it used to be."
Vacations to Busch Gardens, romantic rendezvous' to Aspen,
Orgasms in a heart shaped bed of the honey moon suite,
Plates of pot roast, mouth stuffed with strawberry short cake
On special occasions.
He called me crying, sniveling snot.
"I'm sorry, but I can't see you anymore."
I'm cocooned on the black leather sofa,
Knees pulled to my chest,
Hoping for true love without its crown of thorns.

PISSING

Watch you take a leak
In the mouth of the urinal
Flaps of your jeans folded down
Hand used like a crutch to hold it up
Hung
Golden stream drench
Stroke it a little bit
Let's see it
Don't tuck it in yet
Haven't jacked off all day
Don't zip up
Two more seconds
Shit!

I bought a box of rubbers from Wal-Mart.
I tore off his shirt.
I ran my fingers down his bare arms.
I pulled down his shorts.
I grabbed his dick and sucked his nips.
I stroked his dick.
I kissed his voluptuous lips.
I tongue-tickled the head of his dick.
I couldn't get enough.
I ran my fingers through his punk rock, purple hair.
I tossed his salad.
I squeezed his chocolate ass.
I ran my fingers through the warm trenches of it.
I was so rough.
I clawed at his muscled back.
I milked his dick clean of cum.
I took a whiff of the poppers he offered.
I took every pissy drop.
I ate that dick teaser's ass.
I tapped my foot and got a blow job for it.
I sucked and fucked until he came.
I wanted him to show me his hard on for a blow job.
I want to walk barefoot through a bathhouse.
I want a raving mad scat queen.
I came on his back.
I was shocked when he told me he was only seventeen.
I want to drink sweat from James Franco's T-shirt.
I want to meet the artist who drew this dick on the stall wall.
I was surrounded by a gang of college boy hard-ons.

I want it to rain semen.
I want a man with an asshole big enough to shove a watermelon through.
I was so horny, I licked the urinals.
I just bought a hot-pink dildo and I can't wait to try it out.
I want you to come on my face and stomach.
I got a thing for water sports.
I got a spit fetish.
I unbuckled his belt.
I pushed my hand down his suit pants.
I kissed his belly.
I teased his pierced, Latino nips.
I slipped off the rubber before I shoved my dick up his ass.
I felt him hot on top of me.
I smeared on some lube.
I smothered my face between the cheeks of his ass.
I licked precum from his dick.
I kissed it.
I cupped his balls.
I talked dirty to him while he fucked me.
I handcuffed him to the bed.
I am the slut everyone knows on a first name basis.
I was his dirty nigger.
I want a dick ring for Christmas.
I want to be bound and gagged by Catholic priests.
I am as loyal as a prison bitch.
I want a husband to come home to.
I want a big pink dick.
I want to skull fuck you until you're blue in the face.

I want you to look at me as I fuck you.
I want my ass and mouth fucked.
I want to sniff arm pits.
I got a hairy back with a hairy ass to match.
I need a cuddle slut.
I got a dick like a porn star.
I like to be spanked.
I like to be watched.
I like to show it off.
I want to know who's been drilling these glory holes.
I give good head.
I freed his dick out of his underwear.
I jacked him off while he watched porn.
I slathered him with vegetable oil.
I fucked him in a park bathroom stall.
I shoot huge loads.
I'm a nelly bottom.
I grabbed his ass in a crowded bar.
I lost my balance and my foot slipped into a toilet of pissy water.
I couldn't make out his face. The booth was too dark.
I looked into his eyes red with poppers.
I came in his mouth when he told me not to.
I ate his ass so good.
I didn't think I would ever find his apartment.
I came on his face like he begged me to.
I adore bubble asses and tattoos in grungy guys.
I gagged on his dick.
I sat on his face.

I could feel his tongue up in me.
I watched him from the mirror jacking off at the urinal.
I quickly recovered off my knees when I heard someone walk in.
I could see sprouts of pubic hair.
I sucked his fingers among other things.
I descended down the steps of the basement met with the stench of poppers.
I glanced at his dick at the urinal.
I bought him whatever he wanted.
I love my alligator tit clamps.
I scuffed my knees on the bathroom floor of Mc Donald's.
I got so high off the poppers.
I got peanut butter eaten off my dick.
I got so shit-faced I couldn't remember what happened the night before.
I woke up with a sore ass.
I cocked my legs high.
I start my mornings with a good jack off.

SOMETHING DIRTY FOR OMAR

Cute ass snug in gray slacks
Break me off a piece of that
I wonder what he looks like naked
Tongue and cheek
Tongue between his cheeks
Dick deep in
Omar would kick my ass
If he knew I was thinking about him this way

YOU ARE NOTHING TO ME

But a big dick
A set of low-hanging balls
A warm stomach
A belt buckle in the way
You are just a pair of faded jeans
A common shirttail
An elastic waistband among so many elastic waistbands
I don't notice you down here
Can you see me from up there
I'm a head with a fresh new haircut
Hands on hips
A set of wet lips
A stranger
From a smoky bar

KICKING AND SCREAMING

We talk at Denny's over French toast
About how you want to lose weight and get your teeth fixed
Before a serious relationship.

You want to change your life with lypo suction,
Hold bake sales for cosmetic surgery.

But I don't want a supermodel,
Don't need a man from a Nordic Trac Commercial.

Give me nests of back hair
And love handles of steel.

I'll take the blemishes
And beauty marks.

Fuck the air brushed biceps
From a fashion magazine.

I don't need a man with a rock hard ass.
I'll take the onion breath if it's all the same to you.

I love the way your eyebrows
Come together like star-crossed lovers.

The cleft in your chin,
The sofa you threw out

Before your wife served you with divorce papers.
Say what you want.

Cut me with curse words
Sharp as steak knives.

Tell me you don't like this poem.
Complain to your Wednesday

Night friends about me
Over coke and pepperoni pizza.

Don't just stand there,
Look at me when I'm talking to you,

When I'm kicking and screaming
On your living-room floor.

I'll think of the hair dipped in Clairol,
Your astronomical stomach,

The cleft chin and smelly socks
On an otherwise grotesque sofa

And wonder what makes you
So special for 33 love poems.

ARMED AND DANGEROUS

He ignores me in hallways
Treating me like I'm something disgusting and built-up.
He won't return my calls.
He's warned me to stay away.

Treats me like I'm something disgusting and built-up.
He hired these guys to kick my ass.
They warned me to stay away,
But that's okay, I love him anyway.

He hired these guys to beat me up.
"Get lost," one of them said, before he kicked me in the ribs.
But I don't care, I love him anyway.
I know where he lives.

"Get lost," one of them said, before he kicked me in the ribs.
Stuck indiscreet love letters beneath his door.
I know where he lives.
He and his wife are going through a divorce.

I stick indiscreet love letters beneath his office door
Saying what I would do to him if we were alone.
He and his wife are going through a divorce.
I never liked her anyway.

I tell him what I would do to him if we were alone.
"You're a sick fuck," he says to me on the phone.
I never liked his wife anyway.
He says I need professional help.

"You're a sick fuck," he says.
 But I know he loves me.
"You need professional help!" he yells.
"I'm coming for you baby," I tell him.

I know he loves me.
I'm closer than he thinks.
I'm coming for you, baby.
He doesn't know I'm hiding in the broom closet armed and dangerous.

BLACK AND GAY

Blue back pack
Jeans sagging past ass
Turn around & look
See me
Pee here
Opened shirt
Dick limp
Fat in his right hand

LOST LAKE

I see you jacking off in your mini van
I see you two fondling each other through bushes, trees, ropes of weeds
Hairy backed and naked
I see you jogging, glistening with sweat
I see you in your jean shorts, no underwear
Hung dick, bare ass
Kissing behind tinted windows
I see you sunbathing, body glazed with tanning lotion
I see you blowing him behind that pine tree
I see you kneeling in dirt, red haired, freckled chest
Getting it on in the wild
Head buried in his lap
I see you slapping your dick against his tender white ass
I see a cop creeping around the corner.
I see you handcuffed, escorted to a patrol car
Stuffed in a backseat scared and ashamed

TONIGHT I'M ERIK ESTRADA

Tonight I'm wearing panties

I'm a big shooter

I'm a hard top.

I'm a fem bottom

I'm your jack off buddy tonight

Tonight I'm your beefy stud

I'm a muscle daddy

I'm an afternoon delight

Tonight there are no strings attached

I'm a Queens encounter

I'm a bear always on the prowl

It's time for a blow job

Tonight I'm looking to eat ass

I want some sensual body work

You will find me at all downtown clubs

I'm just a college student looking for fun

Tonight I'm that fun hang out buddy

Tonight I'm a horny bachelor

I'm an Asian hottie

I look like George Clooney

Tonight I'm Donnie Osmond

I'm Erik Estrada

I'm looking to worship big dicks

I'm handsome with a big cock

I am adventurous and open minded

Everyone gets no hassle blow jobs

I'm a black top with 9 scrumptious inches

Tonight I'm not married

Tonight the wedding ring comes off

I am old fashioned, yet modern
I'm looking for a Japanese boyfriend
I'm looking for a sugar daddy to fill me up
I'm boyfriend material
Tonight I'm a medical school slut
Tonight I'm Greek and new to the city
I'm experienced and well-hung
I'm a show off
It's my first time and I'm cute as hell
Tonight I'm looking to $ervice you completely
Tonight I want my ass filled
I'm your body shaving buddy
I'm a loving guy with a juicy dick
I got a thin rod with a mushroom head
Tonight I'm looking for bisexual fun
I only want a discreet relationship
Nobody's perfect
Let's fuck tonight
Let's play
I give free sensual erotic massages
I got a big thick dick
I got a fat man-pussy
Tonight I want to suck young fat cock
I want a jock
Tonight I want someone nerdy and sexy
I want to sniff used underwear
I'm a park slut stalker
I'm a transgender French maid
I suck and lick

Tonight its full service for all midtown boys
Tonight it's free dildos for everyone
I got an ass you won't believe
Tonight I will jack off in front of you
I'm a bi fem
I'm a walking g-spot
I'm your Asian masseur
Tonight I'm available exclusively for you
I give great phone sex
I'm cute with a little baby fat
I want it now tonight
I'm a dick-craving maniac
Tonight I'm a dick-needing daddy
I'm young and black in Brooklyn
I'm clean cut and uncut
Tonight I will massage your ass
I am your disease free top daddy
I'm a hairy chest German
Tonight I'm looking for fast fun
Tonight I'm wearing nothing but a jock strap
Tonight I'm in all places at once
But tomorrow I won't remember your name.

ANGRY SESTINA TO CHRIS

Dear, Chris
I am so sick of your shit.
Why is it that every time I call,
I get transferred to your voice mail?
It either says you are unavailable
Or on the phone, neither of which is true.

Guys like you can never tell the truth,
Got an answer for everything, Chris.
Stop telling me that you will let me know when you're available.
You never do. If it's one thing I can't stand it's bull shit,
Okay? So did you get my letter in the mail?
Why is it that you never call

Me? I call and call
You, but you don't answer. Is it true
What they're saying about you and mail
Order brides? I wouldn't be surprised, Chris.
I'm tired of your shit
You know that? When will you be available

For me to come over and suck your dick? I'm available
On Monday. I know you're off on Mondays, but whenever I call
Your nowhere to be found. Just cut the shit,
Man. You said you had to work but that's not true.
I saw your car in the parking lot, Chris.
What's up with that? You know how much I like you. Check the mail.

I wrote you another love letter yesterday. The mail
Should have been delivered to you by now. *Big* is available
At Border's. I was going to buy it for you, Chris,
But you're such an asshole when I call.
I know the things they say about you aren't true.
I know you just want me to leave you alone, but screw that shit.

I'm crazy about you. That's why I put up with your shit.
I like sucking your dick. I mail
Love letter after love letter to you. I'm true
To you. You were more available
To me when we didn't know each other. I call
You sometimes just to hear your voice, Chris.

I can't help it it's true
What I feel for you, Chris. I wish you were available.
Fuck the phone calls and the love letters.
I have decided to get more aggressive.

HE SAID HE WANTED TO GET NAKED WITH ME

He pulled me like a gun, point blank to his lips.

He groped my nipples.
"Show me those titties," he said.

He stroked me in the bathroom mirror.
My ass angled over assuming the position.

He crouched to my crotch,
Spit trickled to the base of sensitive skin.

Just when I'm about to explode like a Texas oil rig,
He zipped up, washed hands and never looked back.

INVISIBLE

Belly hangs over my belly,
Face fatter than a bowl of grits,
Bologna tits
In a shirt peppered with white stars.

I'm not pretty like the cis white twinks
Who see clean through me in balmy night clubs
Where the floors are slick with tears from plump black boys.

These men don't cut me liquored smiles
As I sit idle in a corner with top shelf whisky on my breath
And sin-stained hands.

SUCK MY DICK

Before my mama comes home.
Daddy just went up the street

For the paper and a cup
Of coffee from the corner Circle K.

Roll on that ribbed rubber for my pleasure
And suck my dick.

Take off your jeans, pull off that tee shirt
Heavy with sweat and give me head.

Suck my dick on the hood of my Ford Ranger.
Pin me to a pine tree.

Take down your Hagger slacks
And see them drop to your ankles.

Eat my underwear and suck my dick.
Forget your wife waiting for you

In front of the tube watching Wheel of Fortune.
Suck my dick.

Get on your hands and knees.
Here are my legs camped

On your shoulders.
Open your mouth and suck my dick.

Suck me in the back seat of your Isuzu jeep.
Suck my dick in these thick trails of mud and mosquitoes.

Don't worry about your girlfriend.
She doesn't have to know. Get down here and suck my dick.

FLESH

Come here in your cut-off shorts
Caramel- colored cowboy boots

A freckled face
Full lips pressed against moon-hued cheeks

Gap between your teeth
Hairy feet
Balls and shaft

Nest of curls between fingers
Ripe nips
Elbow grinds into my stomach
As we make love.

JAIME

Is that you in gelatin-silver print
Sitting on a hardwood bench?

You know if you sit on hard surfaces
Long enough, your dick will fall asleep,

But if you get up and walk it off a little,
The feeling comes back like an ex-boyfriend

Who didn't know what he had until
He packed his shit leaving nothing

But dirty dishes and a drawer full of condoms,
Extra sensitive for your pleasure.

ANDY

I could have done without
The alcohol on your breath.

It wasn't necessary to tell me
How many beers you had

Or how good-looking the bartender was.
I've seen types like you before
With your letter jackets

And sports cars.
Piss drunk in small town bars,
Bragging about how you're going to be a cop.

I don't care that you were an all-star quarterback
With prom queens hanging
Off each shoulder like trench coats.

Guys like you used to pick on guys
Like me when picking on fags made you feel like a man.
What would people say if they knew you play for my team?
A water boy queen warms the bench.

Shower rooms were your excuse to take a peek
At teenage asses. Watch your friends
Whip up a good lather.

Things would have been fine
If you weren't under the influence
Of Budweiser.

Slurred words on your cell phone.
Nodding off in stadium seats.
You grab my crotch in a dark theater.

You owe me a clean hotel room
With spotless sheets.

I want the porno tapes back.
Forget you ever met me,
Lose my number.
Your fake British accent has worn off
Like a hard-on.
Maybe I'll keep the ticket stub
To remember you by
Along with your Budweiser breath
On my chocolate chip nipples.

PACHINKO POEM

Joe, don't take this the wrong way.
Please don't be offended,
But what sorts of things have you stuck up your ass?
Let me ask you this, Joe.
Have you ever stuck a toy car up your ass?
Have you ever stuck a metal brass plated frame up your ass, Joe?
Have you ever shoved a suction cup with a metal hook on it up your ass?
What about a 4 watt light bulb
Have you ever shoved a 4 watt light bulb up your ass?
Or a Suncatcher key chain up your ass?
What about a tennis bracelet or a porcelain doll?
Have you ever stuck those things up your ass?
Have you ever stuck a lock pick up your ass?
Have you ever had pepper spray and said, what the hell,
                                      and shoved the pepper spray
Up your ass?
Have you ever shoved a stun gun up your ass?
What about diamond cut figurines or a 4 pc. Canister set?
Have you ever shoved a pair of cuticle clippers up your ass?
How about a driving mug or some double palm gloves?
I've stuck some candleholders and oil warmer up my ass.
How about you, Joe? Ever stuck oil warmer up your ass?
Do you know what a porcelain papoose feels like up your ass?
Have you ever stuck a hand painted mandala up your ass?
There's nothing I love more than shoving hand painted mandalas
And porcelain papooses up my ass after a long, hard day.
Joe, what about a Casio watch?
Have you ever shoved a Casio watch up your ass?

Have you ever wondered what a skullcap would feel like shoved
                                                  up your ass, Joe?
I have had all sorts of things shoved up my ass
From fingers and frozen breaded fish sticks to herpes dicks and dildos,
But that's another poem.
Have you ever stuck a plant stand up your ass or a hobby tool up your ass?
What about a six foot whip? What about a banana-yellow bandana?
Have you ever stuck a back scratcher up your ass for scratching backs?
Imagine being home on a Sunday afternoon with nothing to do
But just shove things up your ass.
I'm gonna stick a stink bomb up my ass and once that is snug
                                                  like a rug up my ass,
I'm gonna stick a scented rose up my ass and a ninja sword,
                                                         and a beer bottle
And a box of matches and a porcupine and a crystal candy
                                                      jar and a drink coaster
And a table fan all up my ass.
What sorts of things do you stick up your ass, Joe?

DOUG

You don't know that I'm watching you,
Your face seen through the vision of a poet's eyeglasses,
You sketched in notebook indentions.
Reach past a glass of watered down strawberry soda,
A plate of chicken bones
To the telephone to dial your number.
"Is Doug there?"
"This is Doug."
I stop sweating and no longer wish you were not home.

LATE LAST NIGHT

We were two men sandwiched between The Blonde Iguana Salon
And a Park Avenue church.
I couldn't see a thing, but I could make out his Billy club of a dick
Beneath the purplish-white street lights.

I reached into his shorts like a box of Cracker Jacks and pulled out my prize.
Could feel it beat in my hand. I devoured him like I was at an all-you-can-eat
                                                                Buffet.
He was this skinny white boy whose name I never got.

His naked ass was pressed against the Lord's house.
His orange shirt kept dropping like a curtain in my face.
"Suck that dick," he said.
He played with my nipples like toys. His dick was a gun shoved in my mouth.
He blew my brains out.

CUTE MIDDLE EASTERN BOY

Cute Middle Eastern boy you are such a hot piece of ass.
Cute Middle Eastern boy with your ass crack exposed.
Cute Middle Eastern boy you make me so horny.
Cute Middle Eastern boy will you take my virgin ass?
Cute Middle Eastern boy push me down upon my knees.
Cute Middle Eastern boy in your cargo shorts, dark blue T-shirt.
Cute Middle Eastern boy with sweet toes in sandals,
  your lips greasy from Chinese food.
Cute Middle Eastern boy with your raging hard on.
Cute Middle Eastern boy with your fingers around my dick.
Cute Middle Eastern boy come and sit on my face.
Cute Middle Eastern boy with cum in your moustache.
Cute Middle Eastern boy I want to lick the sweat from your balls.
Cute Middle Eastern boy with your Elvis Presley sideburns.
Cute Middle Eastern boy let me lick your boots.
 Give me your ass, cute Middle Eastern boy.
Cute Middle Eastern boy with your lips pressed against my lips
Cute Middle Eastern boy with your scarred knuckles.
Cute Middle Eastern boy make me your piss pig,
  lend me your nipples for sucking.
Cute Middle Eastern boy look down upon me as I take your dick.
Cute Middle Eastern boy I cannot get the taste of you out of my mouth.
  Tip your inches to my lips.
Cute Middle Eastern boy with your dick sticking out of jockstrap,
   mushroom dick hidden under foreskin.
Cute Middle Eastern boy at me riding my hot-pink dildo.
Cute Middle Eastern boy with your balls swinging at my mouth.
Cute Middle Eastern boy let me taste your tongue.
Cute Middle Eastern boy with your brown dick up my butt.

Slather me with baby oil, cute Middle Eastern boy.
Cute Middle Eastern boy may I suck you hard.
Cute Middle Eastern boy won't you fuck me please.
    Take my ass.
Cute Middle Eastern boy I take it hard down my throat.
    Pound my fat ass.
    Watch me jack off.
    Treat my mouth like a urinal, cute Middle Eastern boy.
Cute Middle Eastern boy I will give you head to completion.
Cute Middle Eastern boy tap your foot for a blow job.
Cute Middle Eastern boy coming in pissy toilet water.
    Come on my face.
Cute Middle Eastern boy staining plush car seat with cum.
Cute Middle Eastern boy make me shoot big loads.
Cute Middle Eastern boy let me tongue-tickle your pink hole.
Cute Middle Eastern boy finger-fuck my butt.
Cute Middle Eastern boy makes me hard in these jeans.
    Press your dicktip against these lips.
Cute Middle Eastern boy let me sniff your armpits.
Cute Middle Eastern boy how low your balls hang.
Cute Middle Eastern boy jizz oozing over my fingers.
Cute Middle Eastern boy bind my wrists with your belt.
    Grind my face in your bushel of kinked pubic curls.
Cute Middle Eastern boy naked and bare to me.
Cute Middle Eastern boy trace my trench with your dick.
Cute Middle Eastern boy with your ass hovering over my face.
Cute Middle Eastern boy gag me with your cumsock.
 Bend me over your knee.
Cute Middle Eastern boy won't you spank my naughty ass?

Cute Middle Eastern boy with your ripe foreskin.
Cute Middle Eastern boy shower me with your liquid gold.
Cute Middle Eastern boy with your dickskin pierced with metal.
Cute Middle Eastern boy work that grease up my butt.
   I want your dick up this black, southern butt.
Cute Middle Eastern boy with your dick dripping with my spit.
 With your dick thick with veins.
Cute Middle Eastern boy will you let me drain your balls dry?
Cute Middle Eastern boy please fuck me senseless.
Cute Middle Eastern boy whisper something dirty in my ear.
Cute Middle Eastern boy allow me to spread my ass for you.
Cute Middle Eastern boy I stroke it hard in your name.
Cute Middle Eastern boy taking deep whiffs from your poppers.
Cute Middle Eastern boy I cradle your bubble-butt in my hands
Cute Middle Eastern boy I suck your pedicured toes.
Cute Middle Eastern boy I want to be your sissy bottom.
Cute Middle Eastern boy I can feel your moustache against my ass.
Cute Middle Eastern boy open me wide with anal plug.
Cute Middle Eastern boy with your balls banging against my balls.
Cute Middle Eastern boy let me at your hot dick, my love.
    Shoot your seed upon my belly.
Cute Middle Eastern boy I will drink every pissed drop.
Cute Middle Eastern boy with your tanned belly.
Cute Middle Eastern boy run your fingers through my pubic fur.
    Pry my legs upon your shoulders, cute Middle Eastern boy.
Cute Middle Eastern boy free your dick from green underwear.
Cute Middle Eastern boy let me throw my lips to your dick.
     Let me smother my face in your butt, let me kiss the shaft.

Cute Middle Eastern boy may I sniff your jock?
Cute Middle Eastern boy may I rim your butt?
Cute Middle Eastern boy spit on my asshole.
Cute Middle Eastern boy with your fingers pressed against my pucker.
Cute Middle Eastern boy I tug at your balls gently.
Cute Middle Eastern boy may I suckle your dickhead?
Cute Middle Eastern boy your dick slides so easily in and out of me.
Cute Middle Eastern boy show me your hard on.
Cute Middle Eastern boy with balls tight in leather dickring.
Cute Middle Eastern boy may I kiss and adore your ass?
Cute Middle Eastern boy with your ass tight in faded jeans.
Cute Middle Eastern boy let me sniff your plaid boxers.
Cute Middle Eastern boy let me go down on you till your dicktip touches
                                                                         my tonsils
Cute Middle Eastern boy will you please call me dirty names while you
                                                                         fuck me?
Cute Middle Eastern boy with your hairless balls.
Cute Middle Eastern boy I want to pick your black pubes off my tongue.
Cute Middle Eastern boy with my thick lips around your dick.
Cute Middle Eastern boy I don't have a gag reflex.
Cute Middle Eastern boy with morning hard on.
Cute Middle Eastern boy my hot mouth enveloping your dick.
Cute Middle Eastern boy jack me off under your bed sheets.
Cute Middle Eastern boy, your cum sticky between my fingers.
Cute Middle Eastern boy feed me your dick through library glory hole.
Cute Middle Eastern boy allow me to lick the sweat from your asshole.
Cute Middle Eastern boy can I kiss your pierced boner?
Cute Middle Eastern boy let's run away together.

Cute Middle Eastern boy lets hold hands.
Cute Middle Eastern boy who is that girl?
Cute Middle Eastern boy where are you going with her?
Come back cute Middle Eastern boy, come back!

POEM FOR CRAIG KILBORN

12:52 a.m.
Eight minutes and counting
Until your face shines on the mini
Personal TV my roommate let me borrow
The TV from my hometown only picks up static
Batteries dead in the remote
I reside in a cable-less building, Craig
With two mice that live under the stove
Eating bread crumbs under the dishwasher

You are sky-high tall
I smell your cologne through the puny speakers
I plant palm trees in the worn hardwood floors of my room
I want to be an audience member
I got to get closer to you than Eastern Standard Time
I want to know what makes you tick
After the applause
After the movie and rock stars have left the studio
Who are you, Craig
I want to lick the stardust from your wing tips
Let's play Yambo
It's time for 5 Questions
Ask me anything
Let's talk baseball between the Imodium AD
And Pace Picante sauce commercials
It's 1a.m. and I'm as ready for you as I will ever be

BLACK PORNO POEM

Black Big Boners
Black Dick to Dick
Black Anal Worshipers
Black Can't Get Enough
Black Man Holes
Black Stroke and Blow Club
Black Cock Buddies
Black Intense Studs
   Hot 4 Black Balls
Black Beyond the Hole
Black Flesh Cock
Black Hairy Dudes
Black Cock Fever
Black Sweet Meat
Black Ass Dreams
Black Huge Dicks
Black Tough Gays
Black Bad Boys in Blue Jeans
Black Dick Lickin'
Black Cum Swapping Comrades
Black Gaping Assholes
Black Hot & Horny Men
Black Bad Boys on Duty
Black Wet Gay Perversions
Black Sargent She-male
Black Sinful She-males
Black She-male Nymphos
Black Cum Shots
Black Hot She Cocks

Black She-males Fuck Better
Black Freaky She-males
Black Sexy She Dicks

    Fucked By a Black She-Male
Black Boy-Girl
Black All Cock Access
Black Tranny Sex
Black Teen Trannies
Black Gay Cocks
Black Butt Fuck Buddies
Black Cock Uncut
    My Black Girlfriend Has a Big Dick
    Sweet Black Boys
Black Gay Domination
Black Nubian Horses
Black Woody and His Peckers
Black Uncut Sluts
Black Man Lust
Black Desperate Horsemen
Black Cock in Me
Black Put it in Your Mouth
Black Kissing Dick
Black Cock Gobblers
Black Tight Ends
Black Small Chicks with Dicks
Black Monster Dicks
Black Samson & the Gladiators

Black Cock Friendly
Black Transsexual Penetration
Black Meat by Sissy
Black Anal Paradise
Black Twinks for Each
Black Taste of Cum
   Kiss My Black Dick
Black Men Among Men
Black Brazilian Hunks
Black T-girl Fever
Black Orgy Frat House
Black Cock Wanted
Black Meat Pipes
Black Ass Munching
Black Cock Fest
Black Men in Uniform
Black 976-Cumm
Black Dildo Voyeur
Black Cock Pleasers
Black Gay Paradise
   My First Black Boy Flick
Black Sex Among Friends
Black Rough Necks
Black Juicy Latin Lady Boys
Black T-girl City
   My Black Girlfriend's a Tranny
Black Splendor in the Ass
Black Taboo Trannies
Black Hot Play Thing

Black Macho Fuckers at Work
Black Gag the Fag
Black Bare Bitches
Black Raw Fuck Tapes
Black Hole Wreckers
Black Big Dicks at School
Black Bareback Cellmates
Black Hung Heroes
Black Fuckers Unchained
    To Fuck a Black Predator
Black Swinging Dicks
Black Hot Holes
Black Hot Jocks, Nice Cocks
Black and Bootiful
Black Bareback Campus
    Eric's Black Raw Fuck Tapes
Black Brutal Tops

WHAT I REMEMBER ABOUT JARRET

I remember when I first saw you. You were wearing dark shades.
  You may have said hello to me, but I paid you no attention.
                                        I wondered who you were.
I remember your curly black hair.
I remember thinking that your lips were very full for a white guy.
I remember stacks of freshly printed out poems on your desk.
I remember when I showed you my three-dimensional dragon journal.
                                                   You took it
  And wrote me a check for sixteen dollars.
I remember wanting to hold onto that check as a keepsake, but I cashed
                                                      it anyway because
  I needed the money.
I remember your great big handwriting.
I remember low quiz scores written in red ink.
I remember you saying something about wanting to stick your dick
                                                        between the tits
  Of some freshman girl.
I remember asking you if you were into fat girls.
I remember us eating sandwiches at Schlotsky's Deli.
I remember your one black toenail on your beg toe. I don't remember
                                                           what foot it's on.
I remember boxes upon boxes of undistributed literary magazines.
I remember a picture of a woman on a green cover eating an apple.
I remember we would call each other every afternoon after classes
    And ask if we "got any hits," meaning did we get any poems accepted
                                            for publication in literary magazines.
I remember being very jealous of your success.
I remember you calling me and telling me that Manic D. Press accepted
  Your debut poetry collection, Monster Fashion for publication, and how

                                                                    excited
    I was for you.
I remember the smell of honey mustard from an empty chicken nugget box.
(I was sure Todd left it there.)
I remember a box filled with fat envelopes of poetry.
I remember walking in on you with your shirt off.
I remember how quickly you put it back on when you saw that it was me.
I remember how sad I was, and how much I would miss you when you left
                                                                    Tallahassee.

I WANT TO BE REINCARNATED AS YOUR JEANS

Torn and discolored.
  My arms will play as your pant leg.
The very mouth I used to suck dick
  With will come as the copper zipper.
My pubes are the very threads that
  Make up the inseam that cuts between
Your thighs. I can feel the joy
  In being a favorite pair of your jeans.
Especially in public bathrooms where
  I'm pulled down relentlessly to those
Creamy ankles. The belt hangs loose
  And limp on floors that look like
They haven't been mopped for months.
  I would fit perfectly at the butt,
And around your 32 inch waist
  Directly below stomach, chest
And a land of freckles.
  And when you're done
Pulling me from each
  Lovely leg before a hot shower,
I shall hang pressed on a wire
   Like I was never worn.

THOSE WERE THE DAYS

I'm thinking of your breaded pork chops,
Slices of Italian sausage in spaghetti.
I miss the way the bathroom smelled after you cleaned it,
Your face creams, perfumes advertised in Manhattan magazines.
I miss your skinned head, your broad shoulders,
The stomach that's not quite where you want it .
I would give anything to have you here
Jabbing me playfully in the ribs,
Poking me like I'm a teddy bear.
I miss watching *Sex and The City*
With you in a William Street apartment we shared
Sucking Chunky Monkey ice cream off plastic spoons.
Those were the days.

PUNK ASS

You are such a punk ass
All anti-social held up in your room
Chain smoking, only coming out to take a piss
To make yourself something microwavable in the kitchen
You big punk ass
With your scratchy morning voice
From all the cigarettes
You like show tunes
What a punk ass thing to prefer
You talk to no one and no one likes you
Come out here and face me like a man you punk ass
If I ever see you I'm going to kick your punk ass
All over this apartment building
Just because you are nothing to me
Nothing but a great big punk ass
Only a wussyboy would leave notes under room doors
Pink, punk ass post-its on the medicine cabinet mirror
About eating his food
So what if I eat your cereal
Drink your apple juice right out of the carton
What are you going to do about it
Call your mommy
Tell the landlord
I don't care. I do what I want around here
You punk ass
I wash my ass with your lavender bath gel
It was me who ate your last frozen fish fillet
I did it to piss you off

Because you are the big punkass I can't stand
I'm going to pulverize you
Stomp you into nothing
You punk ass jerk
You make me sick
More than sick
More than sick could ever make me
You are a great big punk ass
And I'm taking it upon myself to rid the world of you

ALAN

"Put some of this on," I said as I handed him the bottle of KY jelly
"I'm allergic to lube," he said.
I thought I had heard it all.
I picked him up from a junior college bathroom
Where we started out jacking each other's dicks under orange partitions
"What do you mean?"
"Whenever I use the stuff small bumps form on my dick."
He was a brunet with a cute face
We took off our clothes back at his apartment,
A weightlifting set in the center of the living room
"What kind of bumps?" I asked.
"I don't know…just bumps."
I asked if he had seen a doctor.
"Yeah, and he said that it's nothing, and that I should make sure I wash my dick."
Still, I wouldn't let him stick it me.
I let him blow me instead, hovering over my lap like a spaceship.
He came in for a landing, accidentally knocking over the bottle of KY
Clumsy dick sucker.

HIGH SCHOOL EPITHALAMION

Roivernon Adams proposes to Travis Asbell
Travis Asbell proposes to Scott Barber
Scott Barber proposes to Michael Brack
Michael Brack proposes to Ryan Bruce
Ryan Bruce proposes to John Brice
John Brice is marrying Lee Conner
Lee Conner is marrying Aaron Carroll
Aaron Carroll is marrying Jason Casseaux
Jason Casseaux just married David Chaffin
David Chaffin just married Michael Chapple
Michael Chapple just married Carlton Crawford
Carlton Crawford proposed to Joshua Cummings
But Joshua Cummings married Fred Davis
Fred Davis proposed to Shawn Davis
But Shawn Davis married Xavier Dempsy
Xavier Dempsy proposed to Dwayne Estelle
But Dwayne Estelle married James Fuse
James Fuse was engaged to Chris Gayre
Chris Garye was engaged to Shay Gibson
Shay Gibson was engaged to Darren Gibson
Darren Gibson was engaged to Shawn Gregg
Shawn Gregg eloped with Brian Gurr
Brian Gurr eloped with Michael Hardy
Michael Hardy ran away with Grady Harper
Grady Harper ran away with Michael Harris
Michael Harris ran away with Moise Harris
Moise Harris was married to Andy Harrison
Andy Harrison was married to Eric Hatcher
Eric Hatcher was married to Richard Herring

Richard Herring said yes to Brandon Houston
Brandon Houston said yes to David Hove
David Hove said yes to Danny James
Danny James said yes to Rashaan Jones
Rashaan Jones proposed to Travis Jones
Travis Jones proposed to Scott Joyner
Scott Joyner proposed to Chad Keen
Chad Keen proposed to John Keillor
John Keillor eloped with Brian Kelly
Brian Kelly eloped with Clint Kinsey
Clint Kinsey eloped with Brent LaBounty
Brent LaBounty ran away with Richard Langly
Richard Langly ran away with Dwayne Lawrence
Dwayne Lawrence ran away with Abe Lerner
Abe Lerner used to be married to Richard Lollie
Richard Lollie used to be married to Thomas Migut
Thomas Migut used to be married to Brian Miller
Brian Miller used to be married to Ed Mock
Ed Mock used to be married to David Moore
David Moore used to be married to Fred Nichols
Fred Nichols is engaged to Shawn O'shields
Shawn O'shields is engaged to Willie Parker
Willie Parker is engaged to Bryan Reed
Bryan Reed ran off with Cleveland Richardson
Cleveland Richardson ran off with Jason Rowland
Jason Rowland ran off with Andy Salley
Andy Salley ran off with David Simmons
David Simmons just married Myron Steen
Myron Steen just married Alvin Tabanguil

Alvin Tabanguil just married Ed Thompson
Ed Thompson proposed to Samuel Towels
Samuel Towels proposed to Anthony Whitehead
Anthony Whitehead proposed to Leroy Williams
Leroy Williams proposed to Titus Williams
But Titus Williams married Russell Wilson

TODD'S WIFE, KERRY

She came stomping through the lobby like a giant.
I thought an earthquake had hit, but in Florida?
Maria, the receptionist, was bleeding from the mouth.
My boss asked, "What the hell is going on?"

I thought there was an earthquake, but in Florida?
She flipped off my boss before she punched him in the face.
"What the hell is going on?"
She was making her way toward me, dragging Maria by her hair like a rag doll.

She flipped off my boss before she punched him in the face.
"Where is he? I'm going to kill him," I heard her scream.
She was making her way toward me, dragging Maria by her hair like a rag doll.
My co-workers feared for their lives.

"Where is he? I'm going to kill him."
I hid under my desk.
My coworkers feared for their lives.
"Tell me where he is and no one will get hurt."

I hid under my desk.
What did she want?
"Tell me where he is and no one will get hurt."
She trampled down the hall like Frankenstein's monster.

What did she want?

"You left these at my house last night."

She lifted my desk like Frankenstein's monster.

She flung my underwear at my face.

I forgot them at Todd's house.

"Stay the hell away from my husband."

"Cheap cologne in my bed sheets."

She lifted me in mid-air and laughed when she saw that I had pissed myself.

RECIPROCATE

I drove past your house
Before heading home
Before a late lunch of homemade slaw dogs
Before doing my math homework
Before writing that research paper
Before writing poetry
Before changing out of my sweaty
  Shirt with yolk-yellow armpit spots
Before rolling on fresh deodorant
Before settling down to a bologna sandwich, grape juice
  And the selected poems of Gwendolyn Brooks
Before calling and saying, I called you earlier but...
Before taking a trip to your office
Before beating off to the mere thought of you
Before checking my mail
Before the evening news
Before a bowl of Raisin Bran now with 25% more
  Raisins
Before taking a shit in the woods
Before taking a piss in my own back yard
Before brushing grape juice stains off my teeth with
  Whitening toothpaste
Before calling friends I haven't heard from in a
  Month
Before writing a single poem about you
Before my wishing you were not married
Before wishing you were as gay as me
Before Jennifer answered the phone, beating you to
  It first

Before the dream of having your dick point blank at
  My lips
Before eating your cum in the identical dream
Before ever thinking of admitting deeper feelings for
  You other than friendship
Before lusting after you like I have with other
  Straight boys in the past
Before cringing as you explain how great pussy is
Before writing you a 16 page love letter
Before sending the birthday card
Before scrubbing my balls in the shower
Before washing my hair with medicated shampoo
Before cleaning out my ears
Before blowing my nose
Before clipping my toenails
Before wiping my ass with flower-printed toilet
  Paper
Before shaving my chest hair
Before shaving my pubes
Before plucking my eyebrows
Before calling and hanging up every time Jennifer
  Answered
Before calling and hanging up every time you
  Answered
Before leaving you 86 messages on your new state
  Of the art answering machine
Before kicking cologne-scented notes under your
  Door
Before buying you a really expensive gift

Before cutting the brake line to your beige Ford your
   Parents' bought
Before slashing the tires
Before busting in the automatic windows
Before caving in the automatic locked doors with a
   Crowbar
Before stumping in the headlights with my steel-toe boots
Before throwing raw eggs at the window of your
   House
Before burning it down
Before stealing your wallet, cutting up your credit
   Cards
Before breaking into your underwear drawer
Before hog tying Jennifer to a garbage truck
   While you watch
Before telling you that I won't be ignored that I will not be dismissed
 Like some field nigger
I decide that if I can't have you, I should move the hell on

WHAT I REMEMBER ABOUT CHRIS

I remember the night we met. It was at X-mart, this store that sold adult toys and videos. There was a sex arcade that had booths in the back where people could go to watch porn.
I remember thinking that you was homeless walking in back with a very thick beard and cap pulled low on your head.
I remember how sore my jaw was after sucking your dick in one of the booths.
I remember us exchanging phone numbers in the parking lot.
I remember not wanting to call you out of being afraid that you would want a repeat performance, and thinking that my jaw most likely would not hold out, but I called you anyway.
I remember your dick growing to be very hard.
I remember your silver PT Cruiser.
I remember writing you love letters.
I remember writing poems about you.
I remember telling you that I was in love with you.
I remember there was a time when you were all that I thought about.
I remember sitting outside of your apartment building in hopes that I would catch a glimpse of you.
I remember sneaking to the back of your apartment and peeking in through the sliding glass to watch you sleep.
I remember buying you DVD's, clothes and giving you money.
I remember seriously thinking about getting Property of Chris Rich tattooed on my arm, or my ass.
I remember a Monday afternoon blow job.
I remember giving you a blow job in my dad's truck.
I remember your black leather sofas.
I remember your apartment on Chapel Drive never ever being clean.
I remember that Dalmatian you had.

I remember when you worked as a manager at Seminole Bowl.
I remember bringing you lunch to work.
I remember sitting in the parking lot waiting to pick you up.
I remember how handsome you looked in a gray suit.
I remember thinking that I would do anything for you.
I remember wanting to kiss you.
I remember giving you a blow job as you drove my car back to your parent's house from Wal-Mart. When I tried to sit up out of your lap, you said, "No, stay down, someone is coming."
I remember the hair on your back that grew in patches.
I remember you telling me that you didn't like soul food.
I remember you telling me that you wished we had become friends first before ever doing anything sexual.
I remember when we went joyriding while we got drunk off Crown Royal.
I remember us eating hot wings and drinking beer at BW3's.
I remember how annoyed I would get when you would strike up a conversation with a complete stranger in the bar about baseball or basketball.
I remember giving you car head in your parent's driveway.
I remember your large collection of porn.
I remember blowing you in your parent's living room. You stripped naked and slipped in one of the porn DVD's I brought.
I remember when Ciara called. I thought how ballsy you were for talking to her as I blew you.
I remember not being very interested when you went on and on about your oral sex skills on women.
I remember asking you who gave the best blow jobs, me or Ciara.
I remember sending you several text messages a day.
I remember calling and always getting your voicemail.
I remember after every argument we had, saying that I would never talk

to you again, yet I never stuck to that.
I remember an instance where I cried on the phone when you told me
that you didn't want to talk to me anymore because
Ciara was getting jealous and angry.
I remember you referring to semen as "nut."
I remember jacking off as I thought of your dick.
I remember swallowing your nut.
I remember when you told me you won ninety dollars playing scratch offs.
I remember giving you a copy of a story I wrote about you. When you told
me that your girlfriend found it, you blamed me.
I remember getting a phone call from a bails bondsman telling me
that you were in jail and you wanted to see me.
I remember how the lobby of the jail smelled faintly of bleach and feet.
I remember going to visit you every day until you told me
that I didn't need to come every day.
I remember that awful blue and white uniform you had to wear
and the white plastic sandals.
I remember wanting to give you everything.
I remember feeling that you were using me, but I didn't much care.
I remember wondering for so long what the girlfriend looked like
and when I found out, I couldn't understand what you saw in her.
I remember you living out of a motel. You refused to pay rent because
the landlord said he wouldn't replace the carpet
after a toilet pipe burst.
I remember fly paper that hung from the ceiling of your bedroom.
I remember Ciara refusing to visit you when you were locked up.
I remember thinking how brave you were for deciding to do jail time
instead of being on probation.
I remember how angry I was that night I saw those two girls follow you

                    into your apartment one late Friday night.
                    You later told me that one of them blew you
                        while the other one ended up passing out.

I remember you telling me to calm down.
I remember wondering why you never called the cops once you figured
                            out that I was stalking you.
I remember getting French Silk chocolate ice cream on my shirt
                            after we went out for ice cream.
I remember how warm your hips felt.
I remember how hairy your ass felt.
I remember you telling me that you were in high school when you
                        began messing around with guys.
I remember you telling me that you were more attracted
                          to Kelly Rowland over Beyoncé.
I remember being quite desperate to have sex with you.
I remember realizing that you were a complete sociopath.
I remember sometimes being repulsed by you.
I remember when Ciara texted me pretending to be you.
I remember seeing your dad and thinking that you look exactly like him.
I remember wondering if your dad's dick was just as big as yours.
I remember your dad being a total DILF. (Dad I'd like to Fuck.)
I remember the only time we could hang out was when
                                Ciara was out of town.
I remember your mom's green minivan.
I remember your dad's old Ford truck.
I remember the long rides out to your parent's house.
I remember after years of being in love with you and obsessing,
                            I had finally snapped out of it.

NEW YORK KICKED MY ASS

Told my friend, Todd over cold salsa and chicken quesadillas
That I'm gonna take a bite out of New York's ass,
But I got lost my first day there. Mama cried on my favorite shirt.
She smeared her makeup as she wiped her tears.
I'll never forget her only words of advice.
"Watch who you drink with." She couldn't shop for shoes in the city
Like she wanted because she was too worried about me.
Her worst nightmare sliced the throat of her nerves like Jason Voorhees.

After unpacking T-shirts and jeans, stuffing twelve years
Of poetry beneath my bunk bed
Like a squirrel tucking away nuts in its cheeks,
I decided to take a tour of the place I would be spending the
                                      next two years of my life.
I walked down the streets that reeked of burnt meat and carbon monoxide
Where young entrepreneurs sold ten dollar watches, incense and boot-leg
                                      blockbusters.
I went to Strand Books for my poetry fix, but all I saw was a cute bald guy
In a black T-shirt sweeping up dust bunnies and wrappers
                                      from snack cakes.

I didn't buy anything.

Drove straight through states and cities the night before,
Survived off chips, candy bars and pineapple soda because for me
It was New York or no place at all, but she's been kicking my ass.
I blew Lady Liberty a kiss, but she never noticed me.
She was too busy shaking tourists out of her tiara.

I got lost four times.

Caught the wrong subway trains that took me to Brooklyn,
The belly of the Bronx.
Native New Yorkers with their Big Apple accents are not as rude
As the rest of the country thinks. They pointed this southern boy
                                        in all the right directions
Telling me where to go and what to do when I get there.
I walked until blisters formed from treading through the Financial District.
New York threw dirt in my face.
She tried to smother me with a Ziploc sandwich bag.
Threw me to the ground in a pitch-black alley, kicking the shit out of me.
New York raped me with a skyscraper strap-on.
The doctor said I almost didn't make it, escaped with some bruising
To the ego, seventeen stitches.

Todd came to visit. He brought me a corn beef sandwich
From Andy's Deli. He said. "You can't go around saying you're gonna
Take a bite out of New York's ass. She's sensitive to that kind of thing.

I Dreamt

I dreamt of getting finger-fucked.
I dreamt of pierced nipples.
I dreamt that my asshole was the size of a tennis ball.
I dreamt of leather cock rings and big pink dicks.
I dreamt I was bound with extension cord, gagged with stinking, sweaty socks.
I dreamt of Jeff Mann raping my butt.
I dreamt I was gagging off his cum.
I dreamt I drank his piss.
I dreamt of frat boy circle jerks. All those dicks coming on my face.
I dreamt of passing my ass around to gang bangers and liking it.
I dreamt of musky white Irish asses and bathhouse floors slippery with semen.
I dreamt of well-hung go-go boys, dollar bills hanging from their g-strings.
I dreamt of Tom sucking peanut butter and cheese wiz off my dick.
I dreamt that I was drenched in piss. I dreamt about the asses of biker dudes hanging out of leather chaps.
I dreamt that my face was being smothered in ripe armpits.
I dreamt of big calloused hands of brutes tugging at my hips.
I dreamt of one big brute dick after another taking it out on my ass.
I dreamt of jacking off with chocolate sauce.
I dreamt of getting fisted by old men.
I dreamt of cum being licked out of the assholes of gay porn stars.
I dreamt of lean, lithe Chelsea boys.
I dreamt of blond fur around assholes.
I dreamt of shaved balls and thick strings of cum in beards.
I dreamt I had a fetish for sweaty, teenage gym shorts.
I dreamt I was getting the best blow job ever.
I dreamt of a butt-plug slathered with Vaseline.
I dreamt that I found a white hair in my pubes.
I dreamt that there was nine inches of dick past these lips.

I dreamt that I got fucked so hard, I began to see stars.
I dreamt of Emanuel's warm asshole.
I dreamt that my daddy caught me jacking off while I watched gay porn.
I dreamt I ate his ass so good, his toes curled.
I dreamt of my lips around his dick.
I dreamt that he was looking down at me smiling sadistically as I blew him.
I dreamt I had a vagina.
I dreamt of the sweet foreskin of Latino men. I dreamt of beefy, bubbled asses
I dreamt of asses with beauty marks, birth marks and asses with freckles.
I dreamt of pimpled ass-cheeks too.
I dreamt of dicks hanging from the zippers of a farmer's overalls.
I dreamt of tear drop piss slits and dick heads glossy with lubricant.
I dreamt of French tickler rubbers and scuffed knees of Brazilian boys.
I dreamt of giving blow jobs in the bathrooms of college libraries.
I dreamt of Dean's sweaty ass.
I dreamt of whips, cuffs and alligator tit-clamps.
I dreamt of wet, naked men toweling off in Montgomery Gym showers,
                        dicks hanging for the attention of a man's mouth.
I dreamt I drugged some Mexican boy and fucked him while he was
                                                unconscious.
I dreamt of dicks being shoved under dividers.
I dreamt of butts cupped in hands as it rode a stiff dick.
I dreamt of that same stiff dick bulging in tight jeans.
I dreamt of hands forcing my head in stinking baseball stadium pissers.
I dreamt of butt-cheeks like valleys.
I dreamt of giving head in the bathrooms of mall food courts.
I dreamt of the warm mouth of a married construction worker.
I dreamt I was getting fisted by Robert Mapplethorpe.
I dreamt of tattooed punks and skater boys with pierced dicks.

I dreamt of cum being spat out in a pool of commode water.
I dreamt of brown teeth from chewing tobacco behind a handlebar
moustache.
I dreamt of dicks sweeter than pussy.
I dreamt of muscular bicycle thighs, cum sticky in crotch hair.
I dreamt of rim chairs.
I dreamt of dick-rings and rappers on-hard.
I dreamt of slurped boners.
I dreamt of sweaty balls stuffed in my mouth.
I dreamt of sugar daddies that would pay me anything for a good time.
I dreamt of daddy- bear dick up my Floridian butt.
I dreamt of enemas filled with a trucker's piss.
I dreamt I was a prison bitch of a white supremacist.
I dreamt of being tied up, slapped around.
I dreamt of him saying, "Suck that cock."
I dreamt of a guy coming through a glory hole.
I dreamt Ma found my stash of porn in my desk. I woke up in a cold sweat.
I dreamt of eating the ass of my American Lit. Professor.
I dreamt of waistbands of boxers showing from the waistlines of jeans.
I dreamt of well-hung insurgents.
I dreamt of giving terrorists blow jobs in exchange for the lives of those on
United 93.
I dreamt of swallowing Bush's poisonous Republican semen
if he would give up the presidency.
I dreamt of sucking off Hitler in order to save the lives of thousands of Jews.
I dreamt of eating his ass if he promised to close the concentration camps.
I dreamt of the sweaty assholes of Iranian soldiers.
I dreamt of drinking piss to save the lives of gay Iraqis.
I dreamt of cowboys in ten gallon hats with ten inch dicks.

I dreamt of a doctor armed with latex gloves exploring my asshole.
I dreamt of semen staining the wedding rings of married men.
I dreamt of offering blow jobs to L.A. gangs in exchange
                                        for automatic weapons.
I dreamt of a hairy ass under panty hose.
I dreamt of balls banging against my butt.
I dreamt I was lying naked on a bed of black leather jackets.
I dreamt of a stark-raving mad scat queen.
I dreamt of James Franco naked on a poster.
I dreamt of shooting off in a white tube sock.
I dreamt of belt buckles clanging against tiled floors.
I dreamt of hands pushed down into slacks.
I dreamt that my dick was thicker than a Kielbasa sausage.
I dreamt of jacking off under my bed covers.
I dreamt of puckered rectums.
I dreamt of stainless steel dildos and chain restraints.
I dreamt of Matt all macho and butch.
I dreamt of being pimped out to dirty truckers.
I dreamt of legs being propped upon shoulders while getting fucked.
I dreamt of all the countless assholes I've rimmed.
I dreamt of video cameras hidden in my bedroom closet.
I dreamt of boys talking dirty to me in Brazilian accents.
I dreamt of nipples bigger than dinner plates.
I dreamt of snorting coke off the torsos of twinks in a Burger King bathroom.
I dreamt of well-hung dicks with lots of veins.
I dreamt that Anthony shot off on my green bedroom carpet.
I dreamt that Bobby and I were high and drunk. One thing led to another
                            and before I knew it, I was sucking his dick.

I dreamt of Michael's country butt.
I dreamt I was fucked up on coke and booze while getting fucked
                                                                                    by total strangers.
I dreamt of pretty light-skinned dicks.
I dreamt of gorgeous Cuban cocks.
I dreamt of puddles of piss on the floors of sex clubs.
I dreamt that my ass was sprinkled with baby powder.
I dreamt of smoke link sausages, bananas, cucumbers, carrots,
                                                           corndogs and dill pickles.
I dreamt my asscrack was wet with spit and sweat.
I dreamt about the muscles of security guards tight under polyester-blue.
I dreamt that I was spread-eagle in the backrooms of leather bars, nameless, faceless men waiting to fuck my butt.
I dreamt that I was bent over a spanking bench, ten to twenty lashes across
                                            my ass with a leather riding crop.
I dreamt of standing in a pit, men gathered around me
                                            and spitting in my mouth.
I dreamt I was puking cum under a plum tree.
I dreamt that I was such a cum-slave.
I dreamt that my tongue was down a drag queen's throat.
I dreamt of nipple rings.
I dreamt that my dick was slathered with coconut-scented hair grease.
I dreamt about hard dicks in smoke-gray warm-ups.
I dreamt about Omair's long, curly hair.
I dreamt I kissed the purple scar above Surachart's groin.
I dreamt I was jacking off to Matty jacking off naked on his bed.
I dreamt of Noel's ass in the air as he blew his boyfriend, Eric.
I dreamt about sniffing Daniel's sweaty shorts after a long jog.
I dreamt about soap lather trickling down into his German pubes.

I dreamt of blowing my professors for an A.
I dreamt about dicks that curved in a weird way.
I dreamt of having phone sex with this guy I went to high school with.
I dreamt that I was getting blown on a park picnic table by a cross dresser.
I dreamt about a young black boy naked on the toilet, jacking off.
I dreamt of old men cruising for dick in stalls.
I dreamt of a single blue eye looking at me through a glory hole.
I dreamt about junior high locker rooms that smelled of ass.
I dreamt about monks naked under their robes.
I dreamt of big-dick Chippendale dancers.
I dreamt of rimming Paul's ass. He was drunk off coconut rum.
I dreamt of sucking off Ishmael in an orange stall.
I dreamt of someone's cum trickling down my arm.
I dreamt of slurping boners.
I dreamt of cum on lips.
I dreamt that I sucked off three dicks in a bathroom infamous for cruising.
I dreamt you took it out on my flesh.
I dreamt of strawberry tongues lapping at musky assholes.
I dreamt I had a dick of death.
I dreamt of dick-cheese curdled in a blanket of foreskin.
I dreamt of fist-fucking, my arm all the way up some guy's ass to the elbow.
I dreamt I was sucking Bryan off in the front seat of my car.
I dreamt I was shrimping toes.
I dreamt I was getting off on the smell of men's underwear.
I dreamt there was something sticky on my belly.
I dreamt of you feeding me Belgian waffles in bed, Matt.
I dreamt of macho butch boys taking it out on my flesh.
I dreamt of a pair of lips that curved just so.
I dreamt of a firm ass in tight black jeans.

I dreamt of gagging off a dick in a dark booth that reeked of fresh cum.
I dreamt about being cock-teased in a gym shower.
I dreamt that I tapped my foot and got a blow job for it.
I dreamt about being surrounded by huge Blatino dicks.
I dreamt that all these men that cruised tearooms, lusted after me
                                        and no one else.
I dreamt about college-age hard-ons.
I dreamt that I was slathered in grape jelly.
I dreamt that I was picking blond pubic hairs off my tongue.
I dreamt that a knife was being held to my throat while being raped.
I dreamt of an ass tightening around my dick. I can't remember
                                        what he looked like.
I dreamt of toothless silver daddies giving me good head.
I dreamt of nappy pubic hairs.
I dreamt of silk panties soft across my dick and balls.
I dreamt of Chelsea boys prying my ass-cheeks apart.
I dreamt of cum dripping from a married man's lips.
I dreamt of blood shot-blue eyes staring up at me, a mouth filled with dick.
I dreamt that I was hung like a donkey.
I dreamt I was a porn star.
I dreamt I could fit two dicks up my ass.
I dreamt of all these men standing in line waiting to fuck me.
I dreamt I was in a hot basement with lots of men, all of them
                                        grabbing at each other's dicks.
I dreamt of an ass that was as white as milk.
I dreamt of a place that stank of poppers.
I dreamt that James Franco and I were fuck-buddies.
I dreamt that I was handcuffed naked to my bed
                                        with an anal plug up my ass.
I dreamt I was slathered in Crisco.

I dreamt that a wrinkled ass was bent to my dick.
I dreamt of wet, sticky fingers traipsing along my lips.
I dreamt of cum trickling down stall walls.
I dreamt that I was being fucked good and hard.
I dreamt that someone was fucking me nice and slow.
I dreamt of a black dildo being shoved up a white ass.
I dreamt I came in Travis' mouth when he told me not to.
I dreamt of big balls in my face.
I dreamt about uncut dicks with mushroom heads.
I dreamt about supple butt-cheeks.
I dreamt that I was pulling some hustler's hair as I fucked him.
I dreamt I was in a porn video sucking dicks to the balls.
I dreamt I was getting gang-banged by she-males.
I dreamt of getting an anonymous blow job in the basement
                                          of an adult video store.
I dreamt of grown men dressed in diapers and bonnets.
I dreamt I was such a slut.

ON DREAMING OF KYLE SECOR NAKED WHEN TERRORISTS FLEW A PLANE INTO THE WORLD TRADE CENTER

I mistook the explosions for lightning.
It had rained the night before.
What the hell did I know about explosions?
Other than what I've seen in a Steven Seagal movie?
Looked out the window in my underwear and R.E.M.
T-shirt to find people running out of nearby buildings,
Down the streets of the Financial District like a herd of circus elephants.
I thought nothing of it until my roommate
Knocked on my double- room door
Crying about six people dead, fifty in critical condition.
Flipped on the TV
Where news anchors were screaming,
"A plane has crashed into the Twin Towers."
A cloud of debris fell over us.
Could smell the blood of the Wall Street work force.
I put on my jeans in fear of evacuation.
My R.A. said we couldn't leave our rooms until further notice.
Stayed put until we were told to converge on the second floor.
But I had not washed my face.
My teeth weren't brushed.
Needed to put on some deodorant.
Wanted my morning bowl of Rice Krispies.
Walked into a cult of frightened freshmen
Panicking in their pajama tops,
Crouching in corners, crying on their cell phones
To parents teddy bear hugs away.
One of the buff security guards from downstairs,
The one with long eyelashes and ass fluffier than yeast rolls,
Was covered in debris.

The contractor assured us we were under a force field of safety.
Stood with my head held high while others sat scared
On the floor biting their fingernails, eating Wheat Thins.
"The other building is still on fire," said a girl wearing an
I Love New York t-shirt.
I was told that we might have to run for cover to Marlton House
Where the beds are screwed to the wall.
Hope the men and women of FDNY are okay.
NYPD blue to the rescue.
Hope the hospitals have enough blood.
I would give them gallons, but I'm not sure if
I'm disease free.
I brought crackers just in case I couldn't
Get to a Burger King or a KFC.
Just in case I had to sleep on cots and eat hard bread.
I didn't want to leave my apartment
Of hardwood floors, marble kitchen counters.
My journals are up there.
My milk is gonna spoil.
The manager from Zetunda brought turkey and veggie sandwiches,
Kiwi and strawberry slushies.
A list was passed around asking those who wanted to stay to sign their names,
And those who wanted to leave could hike up to 14th Street.
"It's like winter outside," said the security guard
With the bubble butt.
We stepped over shoes pulled off in a panic
Making our way to the Graduate Faculty Building.
Human Resources gave us security blankets and pillows.
Some slept in the lounge, conference rooms,

Others in ice- cold hallways, the floors
Of classrooms watching John Waters' Hairspray.
We had full reign over the cafeteria:
Eating barbecue chicken, macaroni and cheese;
Ham sandwiches and cold sodas for lunch
Until we could be placed in alternative apartments.
I could have called my aunt in Queens, but I didn't
Want to put her out.
Slept on a dirty mattress in a Union Square apartment.
Wanted to get out of those three- day clothes,
Wanted to take a shower but their bathroom was filthy.
There were pots in the sink with caked- on food around the rim.
A dinner table of loose papers.
I wasn't used to this much filth.
Finally called Aunt Karen and asked if I could stay with her.
Gave my number to a big legged girl in housing where
I could be reached.
Seamus from 4C wasn't sure if he was going to go home
To Maine where he could play his guitar and eat vegan food
Or stay and sleep, starving on a park bench.
Andy's mom freaked in Philadelphia.
Bridgett from the 8th floor went back to New Jersey and became a prisoner
in her own home. Her mother wouldn't let her leave the house.
I ate steak with yellow rice while watching destruction
Replay on CNN.
Slept like Snow White in my cousin's twin bed beneath
                                          glow- in- the- dark- stars
And an autographed N- Sync poster.
Shaved my head in their blue bathroom.

Returned to William Street eight days later where I was greeted by
Cops and National Guards.
Entered 4B wearing clean underwear to find dust on new poems,
And the burgundy bedspread I'd purchased at Target.
The cleaning crew threw out my milk.
We were told not to use our air- conditioners until further notice.
And here I am after sleeping on the floor,
After being in the same clothes for three days,
After spending the night, showerless on a dirty mattress,
After getting the news that thousands were missing,
And hundreds were found dead,
After the candle lit vigils at fire stations, police stations,
After hearing of Muslims being threatened in their driveways,
After the news of the last dying words on black box recorders,
After the Pentagon was left in ruin,
After seeing pictures of employees in the pages of Newsweek
                                        jumping out of windows,
After Bryant Gumble, Dan Rather,
After Bush referring to Bin Laden as "Hate Monger," "Evil Doer,"
After hearing about New York Firemen, New York Police
Saving mothers, fathers, brothers, sisters, husbands and wives,
After discovering that most of them lost their lives in the process
                                        of such bravery,
After the Red Cross called for blood,
After a generation of young people came to volunteer
Bringing bottled water, work gloves, flashlights and food,
After construction workers and search party dogs
Endured scrapes, scratches and gashes,

After the telethons, the victim relief funds,
After the gathering of Hollywood stars and musicians,
After the postings of missing loved ones have been taped on telephone
Poles, brick walls, the windows of fast food joints,
I still want a bowl of Rice Krispies.

ACKNOLEDGEMENTS

"A Dream," "Black Janitor," "Kiss Me, John Before Your Wife Comes Home," A Married Man," "Bastard," "Something Dirty for Omar," "You Are Nothing To Me," "Kicking and Screaming," "Black and Gay," "Lost Lake," "Tonight I'm Erick Estrada," "Angry Sestina for Chris," "He Said He Wanted to Get Naked With Me," "Suck My Dick," "Andy," "Late Last Night," "What I Remember About Jarret," were all previously published in my chapbook, *Live Nude Guys*.

"Busch Gardens Photo," was previously published in *Nepantla*

Poet, Novelist, Anthologist, Pervert, Homosexualist, Collagist, and Blogger, SHANE ALLISON is the author of the novels *You're The One I Want* and *Harm Done* (Strebor Books). He is also the author of *Slut Machine* (Queer Mojo Press) and *I remember* (Future Tense Book). He lives in Tallahassee.

HYSTERICAL BOOKS
TALLAHASSEE, FL 2019

www.ingramcontent.com/pod-product-compliance
Lightning Source LLC
Chambersburg PA
CBHW020659300426
44112CB00007B/445